TWENTY-SEVEN PROPS FOR

A PRODUCTION OF *EINE LEBENSZEIT*

TWENTY-SEVEN PROPS
FOR A PRODUCTION OF
EINE LEBENSZEIT

TIMOTHY DONNELLY

Grove Press
New York

Grateful acknowledgment is made to the editors of the magazines in which versions of these poems first appeared: *American Letters & Commentary:* "An Autocracy on the Lounge"; "The Ghost of a Flea"; *Conduit:* "An Acting Appendix"; "Birdsong from Inside the Egg"; *Denver Quarterly:* "Ease"; "Her Palm, Her Apotheosis"; "Monastic"; "Vera on Atmosphere"; *Fence:* "From a Further Meaning Faded"; *Gulf Coast:* "Relief in Gestures Artificial and Oblique"; *Jacket:* "Anything to Fill In the Long Silences"; "Dark Night on the Inside of a Rock"; *LIT:* "Known Minutiae"; "Nauseous House"; *Now Culture:* "Sonata ex Machina"; *The Paris Review:* "Bangor"; "His Long Imprison'd Thought"; "The Truer"; *Ploughshares:* "Maintenance"; "Marblehead"; "Scarecrow in Magnolia"; "Self Exhibited As a Wasting Phoenix"; *Quarterly West:* "Isn't It Romantic?"; *Slope:* "Through a Darkness, an Intelligence"; "Pansies Under Monkshood: A Folly"; "Der Nachtschwärmer"; "For a Missing Face"; *TriQuarterly:* "Purgatory Chasm"; *Verse:* "An Inflorescence"; "Anything to Fill In the Long Silences"; "Twenty-seven Props for a Production of *Eine Lebenszeit*"; *Volt:* "Delphinium"; "The Driver of the Car Is Unconscious"; *Western Humanities Review:* "Accidental Species."

The author gratefully acknowledges the support of the New York State Writers Institute and its grant of a Master Writer Fellowship during the summer of 2001.

Published simultaneously in Canada
Printed in the United States of America

FIRST EDITION

Library of Congress Cataloging-in-Publication Data
Donnelly, Timothy.
    Twenty-seven props for a production of Eine Lebenszeit / Timothy Donnelly.
        p. cm. — (Grove Press poetry series)
    ISBN 0-8021-3957-4
    I. Title: 27 props for a production of Eine Lebenszeit. II. Title.
PS3604.O636 T85 2003
811'.6—dc21   2002033862

Grove Press
841 Broadway
New York, NY 10003

03   04   05   06   10   9   8   7   6   5   4   3   2   1

For my mother and my father

CONTENTS

FOREWORD

First things first: readers necessarily unfamiliar with the new poet's work will gape at the odd title, which means no more than a plethora of supports for the performance of an imaginary play—the allegorical rendering of an entire life (*Eine Lebenszeit* = a lifetime). Fair enough, if winsomely arbitrary—any other title in the collection is just as likely, as likeable. My own choice takes after another poem, "Accidental Species," which embodies just as many clues to the name and nature of the remarkable poetry Donnelly writes.

This poetry is as vigorous, as fresh, and as authoritative as any new work I have seen since Ashbery's third book. There is a filiation between Donnelly's work and Ashbery's, but it is a matter to be treated briskly, without too much heavy breathing (I speak for myself here—Donnelly's respiration is ever light, ever lively): Ashbery has come to be known for poetry that refuses to emerge from its rhetoric, its various registers of diction, and its apparent lack of immediately identifiable subject-matter.

Donnelly's too is a poetry of words rather than of stories or characters, but where Ashbery treats his nomenclatures with a certain dryness, Donnelly is exuberant. He is a logomaniac, and every poem coils about its syntax like a sleek python of reticulated verbality:

> I was a plaything to the climate, the breezes
> lifted, swept me vast and plastic as they
> wished, all eyes to my assignment from
> the power in whose eyes all palaces, pyramids,
> and the worms that build them are alike
> contemptible; I was a humble ship set
> hazarding from rock to rock, and on each
> I struck a wreck, and all that changes you, confuses
> parts for wholes, so that you become
> the very swarm you would dismiss but can't
> because it's you . . .

This is, I submit, the poet on himself and his venture, and a good example of Donnelly's Way: it is not quite narrative, and not quite lyric—permit me to call it epic meditation, a poetry of engagement with the various levels of Being that can be summoned up by words from the different registers that the poet commands or, more likely, command him.

I believe this work to be as handsomely delivered as any to be found in new American verse—indeed, the differential point with regard to Ashbery is that Donnelly is always sensitive to the line, the stanza; he never ignores the responsibility of form. Hence the elegance of even his most extended pieces, carefully disposed within the demands of the various rhetorics Donnelly has assimilated:

> . . . I am by nature
made a mimicker, by miracle adept at taking in
and flinging back . . .

This young poet clearly identifies his agon when he asks himself: "Will we be the masters of the art, or its victim?"

The entire book is the answer, but an answer always in dispute. I am perfectly aware that the first (and probably last) question that will be asked is "What's it all about—what's he saying?" The poet too is conscious of—and agonized by—these interrogations, as when he has his Miss Singleton, author of a *New Deportment Manual*, ask:

> "Why not use appropriately varied tones of voice
so that each individual might best be able
to harvest the pleasure of your company?"

and he eagerly and immediately answers her:

> I do. Or I would. That is I will. I feel
relieved *and* anxious, as when discovering
the source of life's mysterious scratching
is a colony of ants beneath the wallpaper.

Miss Singleton, call a doctor. There's disease
about the mouth. It is ashamed of itself.
It makes noises that don't ever belong . . .

And this wonderful poem, a sort of *ars poetica* that is also a bit
lover's complaint, concludes with the heartbreaking line: "The ter-
ror I inspired I am made to feel."

Perhaps that is the ultimate point to be made about Donnelly—
he has the true resonance of heartbreak, the *lacrimae rerum* note
in all his extravagant address, his goofy transformations ("I would
like being a bird, just not a raptor, except perhaps / an owl"), his
intricately detailed nature-studies:

Windowed, he will watch
an autumn's fancy branchwork, the crocus spitting gold-
dust stigma-tassel (saffron), but mourn the patch
of purple browning by the brick, the offal-air of mold
and loveless decomposing. Chiller nights approach.

Note the careful rhyming, which helps us into and through
the big pieces, the music sounding where the meanings appear to
rescind. I must not quote more; instead, I urge a reading of this
brilliant (and unabrogable) book. It demands to be read *as poetry*—
not as social studies, psychiatry, or even wardrobe boasting. It will
be a pleasure as well as a privilege for readers attentive to contem-
porary poetry, and I am quite convinced that the poet has such
readers in mind with the final words of one of his finest poems,
"The Spleen's Own Music," when he says:

You approach me for an answer. I hand you
what you want. You have been given another life.

—Richard Howard

The delight I take in my thoughts is delight in my own strange life. Is this joy of living?

—Ludwig Wittgenstein

ONE

TWENTY-SEVEN PROPS FOR A
PRODUCTION OF *EINE LEBENSZEIT*

Let there be *lamps* of whatever variety
presents itself on the trash heaps. Let chance
determine how many, but take pains
to use only low-watt bulbs, and keep the lion's share
flickering throughout the performance.
In particular, one gooseneck should pulsate religiously
on the leeward corner of an *escritoire,*
which is a writing table, or an unhinged door

suspended on sawhorses. These will be spattered
in a clash of pigments, signifying history.
Dust is general over all the interior.
You are very tired. You are very weary.
On the floor, one *carpet,* its elaborate swirling
recalling the faces of wind on old maps.
And let there be *maps,* at least half reimagining
the world according to a scattered century:

a shambles, patched. Now for the *wall-clock*
which hangs prodigiously over every act. Let's rig it
so the hour revolves in a minute, the minute
in a blur. Grab hold of an enormous *mirror*
and mount it divinely—that is, too high to bear human reflection.
And what do you call it when you can't endure
the scraping of the blades of all creation?
There'll be a *bucket* of *that,* another for the *suet,*

a third marked SESAME but filled with *sand.*
Place this last a judicious distance
from the bamboo *cage* in which one *ostrich,* plucked,
stands Tantalus-style, its beak eternally
approaching the rim of the third of the buckets.
Does the bird want seed, or is it onto the trick
and terrified, frantic to bury its head in the sand?
Will it never end? But look who I'm asking!

3

Take your worry to the *sofa,* lie there.
There's a pillar of *books* and a French *periodical*
on either side. Before you know it,
it's always midnight. Now the *owl* of Minerva
takes its flight down the nickel wire.
Now a *dampness* pumps from the tightened fist
of a cold *contraption,* a sort of inverse
radiator, and you can't control it, and it isn't pretty.

Tell me you love me. There's a severed *hand,*
or is it a fruit peel? Tell me you love me
and I make it mild. Take your panic to the *sleigh-bed,*
slump there. There's a snatch of *heather*
and a cracked *decanter* on the starboard side.
Before you know it, it's always never.
You know I hate it when you whimper, don't you?
Now shut them big ambiguous eyes.

Now shut that cavernous cartoon mouth—
and here's the *sock* to fill it, periwinkle!
You know I hate it when we don't coordinate.
Now what's that rapping at the shattered *window?*
It's the only egress, I neglected to mention.
But here's a *rope* with knots to help you shimmy down—
a dozen square knots, the last a hangman's.
Now take your heaving to the *curtains,* part.

They're dove gray, dolly, and fall like art.

AN INFLORESCENCE

1.

A rumbling, a spark; an inflorescence—

Aloha, Hibiscus! You glow through the gloam
in the blank of my soiled and grandiloquent
head, from a bed spread fertile with waste
that has waited too long for your purpose, churned
over and over by the seeking worm,
the nocturnally restless. A torment ago,
I made love to a form; I festooned it
with adjectives: beauteous, consummate, dulcet, plum.
A player is forced to make love
to a vagueness, a layer of foam. A torment ago,
I would not have presumed
your aroma, your nimbus, your ruby conundrum, but a riot
develops in the sluggish blood-pump,
and the cleaving of mist betokens a romance.

Hot ukulele! How do you do?
And you: beamy, beamy.

Where do you come from?
What fire, what flood?

What wild effluvium?
Did your kernel pass

through the tract of an auk
as it flew overhead?

You nod to me yes,
but the bird is flightless, pink coquette,

and I can't believe you.

2.

Hibiscus, *mon âme*! You are governed by Venus, ambiguous,
               frilled, and aware of your charm;
          should the governor throw
     a ball you will be there, the mistress
of many, but pinned to my arm.

I know a valley fair,
I know a cottage there
Hibiscus aroon!

A breeze is released
from your tropical pockets
Hibiscus aroon!

Stay, my irruption.
Will others excite you? There's divan enough

for the pair of us only—
and paradise, paradise.

Come to me now with your exclusive stalk,
with your enciphered leaves. There are parts of me

naked and the tambourine grows rust impatiently.
Show me your rootstock, windlass, lavolta; mouth

phrases of fuchsia and the South Pacific into my deeply
attenuated ear. A torment ago, I made love to a form, I festooned it

with adjectives: curious, high-stomached, plausible, smooth.
A player is forced. There's fossil enough to grease any engine,

but a storm develops on the azure plain, but the blathery palms
will drown us out that crowd us in, and I will not release you.

SONATA EX MACHINA

1.

Better to advance. Let the winds of the explosion
whip your pinions into motion, plough a happy

figure forwards into *where*s and *when*s and *how*s
you have no words for *a priori,* but will upon

arrival—however used up from the flight, your inner
dictionary fattens to accommodate the new

accommodations, an appendix on the walls in which
you measure through the noise, in which

much / a dovecote / better to

keep quiet about the whole damn debacle
than to drop any hints and/or bitch about it outright.

The desired machine plays the smallest
sonata possible, an arrangement of gastro-

intestinal blips, and this only at night when the
program at night when the program skips,

when the noxious smokes of another day's traffic
rise off the asphalt and fuck with the

filter you / disposable / change

every morning, absolutely every. The desired machine
will start itself and stop itself, will fuel itself

and fuck itself. It will right itself when thrown
off-kilter, and it will even change its own

damn filter. It would make itself if it had to, but it don't.
That old-fashioned reveling in the general

situation grows less and less plausible as we
uncover the defects of natural laws, and see

the mess we're / perpetual / in and how

one sumptuous decision delivered us thither.
At the steakhouse: yearning for the difficult,

weary of the offered, sick of the appetizer,
hot for the remote; dizzy from the cocktail,

apart from the ambience, tickled by the mishap,
hoping for another; distant in approach

but none's the wiser, sharpened by the entrée,
hot from the cocktail, hoping for another,

nostalgic for / a dovecote / . . . THE APPETIZER!

2.

What are the traits that delineate the human?
Leave   me   alone.   Allegorical, and

with a whore's abandon, Philosophy knocks
at the cinquefoil of the world-side window,

one index bloody from the sticking to it, her dumb
wheeze the wisdom of the ancients, busted.

Having trundled the planet since embryonic,
she's all tuckered out. —Heck, an anchorite's

seclusion's not / excuse me / *contemptus*

mundi necessarily, but a way of making manifest
one's ineluctable apartness from that world

which one would love to be a part of and *immediately,*
but, seeing as that's inconceivable, a wonder

which refusing, given even more technology—
Invite the lady in. She's peddling consolation.

(What wanderlust has wrecked her skirts?
They've ceased to swish that certain way.)

3.
What wanderlust has wrecked your skirts?
They've ceased to swish that certain way,

that distingué, that way they did days halcyon,
what goings-on have been going on, keep

going on, that flounce's flown, that fringe's fled,
once chestnut brown went chestnut red, and now

it's rust, Philosophy, and rusted skirts, they just don't swish.
Your chestnut skirts—

Better to keep quiet.   Corrosion starts
which can't be stopped in the hidden parts—

in the joints, the folds, the seams, the borders.
Carnation, lily, lily, rose. The cloister's moister

than the monks suppose. What grows there rots,
what rots there grows. Carnation, lily, lily, rose.

Whose first demonstration showed that thought
romps with the other diseases of the flesh, whose

second claimed that "ideal physical beauty"
proves incompatible with emotional growth and a full recognition

of "the coil of things," whose chestnut skirts—

Better to advance.   Suddenly 80 percent of all questions
are statements in disguise?   The desired

starts itself and stops itself, fuels itself
and fucks itself. It will right itself when thrown

off-kilter, and it will even change its own
damn filter. Though I wasn't fully present

at the meeting, I am sold. A wonder which
refusing to be useful rose with making me.

A thousand budding clovers pock the public lawn.
Exactly incoherent? That's because I didn't

hear you in the first place, and I myself am
only responding. A wonder which refusing to

be useful rose with making me, as light will
make a window be: a vessel for its beaming.

4.
Listen. Every morning, in seclusion, celled
in bricks as I am bricked in cells, self-

fitted with a morning's filter, humming, I pour myself
a tremendous bowl of breakfast flakes

and let it sit there on the morning's surface
for however long the morning takes, half

an hour, longer, maybe twice, until the cereal
becomes such a confused little swamp

that no known human would ever think
of eating it, and then I take my lump

and eat it, but not out of hunger,
which is the one thing, but compassion,

which is the other, and though it cramps my heart
to tell you so, the music says I must,

and that's where my allegiance is.
Your chestnut skirts do not exist.

What are the traits that delineate the human?

I   am   not   my   own   machine.

ISN'T IT ROMANTIC?

His thought appalled us. It bore the mark of having strayed too deep into the company of others. And what a drastic forest that is. Larchwood, leaf mold, *ignis fatuus;* bandit faces grazing on him on an antique train. And he allows it, yes. Allows each mouth its history of twisting, allows each fist. It's much too hideous to dwell on, sadly. *Only ten more minutes,* he thought, *and I'll be lying softly in my rented dark, almost invisible.* Well, you can see it, can't you— how it bears the mark? He absolutely should have put it this way: "Only ten minutes more. . . ." And what does it mean, that he'll be lying "softly"? We are all of us liars, and we doubt it means anything, anything at all. He has fallen into a habit we abhor, as one might fall from a hotel window ten flights up, the darker throes of rapture, bathrobed. And he has landed "softly" in the crowded bed of a passing truck. (We'll show him "softly.") The truck barrels off. "Crowded" with what is what you want to know. Well, Inspector, that would have to be manikins. Hairless limbs and paint expressions, some kept whole but most discon-nected, all of them naked with the stink of plastic. And look at him scramble just to keep them warm, as if it could matter! (Let's suppose it's snowing.) And when he realizes that he can't save all, he chooses one. She's still intact, though her look is distant. He dresses her up in his hotel robe; he belts it tight. Isn't it romantic? He throws his useless arms around her, throws his worries into her empty head. If you could just for once. (It's forever, get it?) If you could just for once keep your damned trap shut. Isn't it romantic? He chooses one; he belts it tight. The truck barrels off into an endless night. If you could just for once. No one ever talks to us the way he talks; just listen to him coo: "You want me to clear out room for you to sleep in? You want me to see to it nobody touches you?"

DER NACHTSCHWÄRMER

I know a shape that knows its way around
  Our park, whose panther-musked and sparkling coat
Entices—then appalls! It should be chained
  By park officials. All day it lurks about
Unseen beneath the band of evergreen
  That cordons off our curfewed park; it slinks
Among our founding fathers' watching pine,
  Does damage to their sap-filled trunks
    And leaves one ill at ease. Tonight a troop
    Should trap it, bind it up with iron and rope—
  But night is quite a different game, now, isn't it?

I know a shape of such intelligence
  That it waits till night displaces day to spring
From fallen needles. Then it rises, grunts,
  And *bang!* it lunges from the boughs that hang
So low as to conceal it underneath.
  And when it makes it to the lawn, so ticked
It glows below the moon, a grille of teeth
  Is cruelly born; the tongue contorts: you're licked
    With lechery and wet. Tonight a troop
    Should trap it, bind it up with iron and rope—
  But night is quite a different game, now, isn't it?

I know a shape with eyes reflecting stars,
  They mesmerize! whose quick-seducing gaze
Will bore through barriers and barriers:
  You fill with thoughts much less your own, your knees
At once begin to buckle, and you fall beneath
  The shape; ah! life's unlucky. You breathe and bleed
Its breath and blood, now intertwine a leg with
  Legs and wake up in a spill upon the bed.
    You'll wish it had been stopped. Tonight a troop
    Should trap it, bind it up with iron and rope—
  But night is quite a different game, now, isn't it

13

About to start: a theater of puckered whelps
   And pathogens from humming pumps, a secret door,
A sodden hall, a carousel of shadow palps
   Divining where the flattered vein begins. You're
Swept away by caravan, you're miles from an old concern—
   What was it once, an emptiness, a ticket?
With another fume, another face, another turn
   In the sticking-place with silver-tongued constrictors in the socket,
      Odd cologne! And now, with rumbling, comes a troop
      To bind you down (or is it up?)
   And you allow it as the shape assumes your own.

MARBLEHEAD

The first item up for bid: a charming new gazebo.
It's made of wood that smells like wood that smells
like gunpowder. Like everywhere, it is a place to sit.
But this is different. I mean, you put a cat in there,
and before you know it—catheter. I think I didn't say that right.
Fantastic night: a sitting there. A fantasy. A sweet
old-fashioned fantasy for your ass to slip away to.
Just think of it. For example, kick back and drink
that damned Bordeaux you can't shut up about. This is what you get.

The second item up for bid has more to do with music.
Listen, why the argument? What's musical to me
might be a battle cry to you, the blue . . . —You didn't
let me finish. What's musical to me: the bluest
banjo bleeding red, and then to sleep another hour.
But what if "has to finish"? —You didn't let me flower.
But what if "Marblehead"? Suddenly it isn't funny anymore; that ol'
gazebo ain't ashake with braggy laughter. Suddenly
it is I who should be burying the hatchet, not vice versa.

The third item up for bid: a dachshund named Hephaestus.
Isn't that a scratch? Of course it is; he's restless.
It looks like he's forging an armament, but he's not.
He's only digging. Today's his whole month off.
Hot diggity! Like his namesake, Hephaestus hates his job,
hates the "have to" part of it. When you scratch
behind an ear, he says, "Against my will, no less
than yours, I must rivet you with brazen bonds."
He thinks that you're Prometheus. This is automatic.

The fourth item up for bid belongs to you already—
technically, technically. In fact, not long ago you thought
you couldn't live without it. A little piece of you-
know-what we cut from deep inside your thingamajig. Any bright ideas?

Clue #1 from G. E. Lessing: "I am a long way
from seeing the object itself." Sound familiar?
Clue #2 from "Little Gidding": "There are three conditions
which often look alike / Yet differ completely."
Sound familiar? Sound enticing? Guessing's over. End of bidding.

The final item up for bid is just about to happen.
The year: 1770-something. Your name: Colonel John Glover.
The 14th Mass. Infantry is under your command.
Kapow! You are now highly respected by George Washington.
Kapow! Your strategic skills and that crackerjack
leadership just earned you a promotion to general.
You are to answer truthfully: Do or do you not love love?
What will you sacrifice? Are you willing? You are
invaluable throughout the revolution, Mr. General,

and critical in three instances. Quick, you are bleeding.
Ticktock, ticktock. Ain't nothing in the world
like the confidence a stopwatch gives you, don't you find?
Ticktock, ticktock. Say good-bye to that new gazebo!
And I'm not talking the kind that fits like a pack of mints
in a seersucker pocket. Say good-bye to that generalship,
to that you-know-what and all that music. I'm talking big. Look,
the many lights of your showcase spectacle blink and fade
like the tired eyes of an inner monologue! But where's Hephaestus?

Down in the hole that digging made. I'm talking enormous.

FANNY FOWLER'S POETRY AND DIORAMAS WORKSHOP

You can ride high atop your pony
I know you won't fall . . .
'cause the whole thing's phony.

This is the forest primeval that Jack built.
This is Jack's first-ever poetry diorama.
This is papier-mâché, crepe paper, clay—
a good kind of clay—felt and three velvets
arranged in a tribute to Longfellow.
This is the forest primeval in a shoebox.
A girl figurine stands glued in the hollow, an Evangeline
of the five-and-dime, unable to follow
the workshop participants who, as they murmur,
murmur like pines and like hemlocks.

—But they are warriors all, floored
warriors whose veins engross a richer purple.
(I had a need in winter. We all did, oh.)
Jennifer's "Rape of the Lock" diorama
raises spirits and questions of gender: zeugma!
(I lost myself inside me. We all did, oh.)
The "Goblin Market" Donna made is dizzy
with fruits overwhelming a marzipan Lizzie.
(I had a need in winter. I don't care how.)
Nathan never esteemed *The Waste Land* so much as

making his own heap of broken images
and this is the forest primeval that. . . .
—Jack's overcome a great many setbacks; back
in New Brunswick, what absolute zero!
—bunched like Quebec, Nova Scotia, Ontario,
and Jack's overcome a great many hurdles
that heaved up before him like woodlands or mountains
that dropped down upon him like curtains

or turtles that came at him sideways like bullets that fly
through the indistinct twilight of Canada.

"However," says Jack, "I was born in New Brunswick,
New Jersey. People say I worry too much,
but that's because deep down I'm a perfectionist.
Sciences excite me, but my true love?
You guessed it. I have a need to express myself artistically,
I don't care how. I joined the Drama Club
in school, wore my scarf inside in winter, we all did. Summers,
I closed a donut shop near Rutgers, then *poof!*
I'm a Junior Executive. Big business is mysterious.
Last year, I lost my cat Mephistopheles
                             to natural causes."

Natural causes! The very phrase is like the punch
   That made the birthday boy puke up a very
Sudden mess upon Felice, whose lunch
   Of turkey breast on wheat with a little cranberry
Sauce on the side, please, thank you, shot
     Up her bent esophagus and got, well,
       Lodged there. Funny how, in all that flight
         To save Felice, no one thought
      To call the causes natural. But they *were* natural,
        Weren't they? Am I right or am I right?

Anyway, Felice demands attention, and all
   She demands she gets. Touchy little Fanny,
Ten at the time, doesn't think a small
   Lapse in peristalsis justifies cacophony
On this level. Moreover, Fanny wants
     Another cupcake, and this time make it lemon.
       (Nothing.) Fine, she'll get it herself.
        But don't think she, I mean, this experience,

Don't think she'll forget it—she can't! Its demon
   Has possessed her ever since. And not its elf,

mind you, but its demon. Today, Fanny cuts
a spellbinding figure throughout most greater
metropolitan areas. Her phenomenal success,
however, was (in her own words) "hard-won."
Fowler's mother's byzantine neuroticism
and her father's reluctance to address her directly
cast a pall over every minute of her youth.
As a retreat from this dark, haunted, and
(in her own words) "quite possibly convulsive" atmosphere,
Fowler turned to poetry at the age of

twenty-eight. The rest is literary history.
Among her sharper innovations, Fowler's infamous
"Poetry and Dioramas" workshops perhaps
pierce deepest, rivaling in radiance the sloe-
opening eye of Cleopatra's asp. Just ask Jennifer.
Just ask Nathan. Just ask anyone lavishing today
in her essential air, where all that's rigidly
poetical at last relaxes. This is the Belle of Amherst's hearse.
Here's wee Robbie Burns in a windblown kilt.
This is Pandemonium, and this is *The Bridge,*

and this is the forest primeval that Jack built:
A twenty-first-century three-dimensional
fastidious faux-naïve mixed-media
expressivist "manifestation" of a cherished
American Renaissance dactylic chestnut
epic in which the words *sickness, horror,* and *dread*
each appear exactly once, and in which
the words *empty, vacant,* and *mocking*
each appear exactly twice. —Jack holds his handiwork
up before the workshop. The warriors

are restless. They enumerate the greenery's
many greens (seven); they note their drawn reflection
in the little mirror lake. Under artificial light,
it's impossible to tell where Jack went wrong, and yet
the warriors are restless. Something's missing.
They say, "He isn't fighting with the medium."
Jack admits that he in fact forgot to, having lost—
They say, "He has the pugnacity of an empty
glass of old what-have-you, the jaw-drop of an ass
whistling at the foot of a painted mesa."

What happened? A cloud of resentment over-
shadows the gallery of best intentions.
Biochemically speaking, a paranormally high
register of psychic excitation has, it seems,
been generated by the workshop's various
material stimuli in combination with a built-in promise
that no diorama can ever live up to, creating
an emotional storm center that everyone and her grocer'd
do well to avoid. Donna has a point when
she blames herself for the day's disappointment, for

it was she who raised the specter of _____. The possibility
of further commentary slumps from the scene
like a broken dromedary. Jennifer: "If you fashion
that selfsame image out of clay, a good kind of clay,
then it will stay that way forever, perfected, whereas
language is never the same thing twice, and perhaps
Jack's vision isn't yours, or mine, or anyone else's."
Nathan: "No, that can't be right. Strike that passage
from the record, thank you." Everyone remember *The Manager's Tale*:
"Once upon a time, there was a great importance,

Only nowhere to place it, so we threw it out."
—Inwardly, Jack considers the link between that celebrated
"Disposal" and his own "disposition" without
    Realizing that the words aren't really related,
Derivationally speaking, but such is the chatter
    That cheers the warriors who, however shaken,
        Keep thinking that some special thought they think will
            Somehow matter, that some matter
    They manipulate might make tonight's Hoboken
        Stars embark upon a deeper twinkle.

A deeper twinkle! Who among us hasn't
    Stridden night's innumerable planks and almost
Poked head through those high effervescent
    Nimbi curtaining the ultimate answer's ghost-
Gazebo's twenty-five thousand pinprick windows—
    Only to lose it all on a slip, a blinking. All's storybook
        Letdown, why deny it. "Darling, I have often,"
            Starts one to the other, "and it all blows
    Over," ends everyone, breathless. The diorama: a gridlock?
        No, not that. The diorama: a coffin?

No, not so. Tell us, Fanny, with your gravy-
boat delivery and love in every lump, what's it all about,
what's of any real value now that the wheezy
water-pump in the town's sad center—whose water once
hissed down red-hot throats—has pumped out
nothing but a cobweb for a century at least, and we,
adaptive, have grown accustomed to that empty
gossamer which, however tickling, seldom satisfies
and will never nourish? No, not us. Our mouths,
our cardigans hang upon a vestige. Fanny, speak!

[With gravity]

When I look around this room, I see a lot
of dioramas. I mean a LOT of them. I really do.
And THESE dioramas are REAL dioramas.
They really are. And I KNOW that you MADE them.

[A flock of peacocks lifts her hem.]

And I KNOW that you MADE them TODAY.

CHANCE OF INFINITY IN A LITTLE ROOM

1. THE GHOST OF A FLEA

*after William Blake: tempera heightened
with gold on mahogany, c.1819–20*

Consciousness, is it? I had thought myself
finished, released from the rig,

the indelicate rigor. I remember admitting
the blank as the drowning

must welcome the water
at last, "At last, I am done

with the thrashing now
bent on solution." Infamous process!

The old washes off, and you
break in the new: I was hurled

through a weed with no tender to speak of;
no cushion, no salve—and already

the stung tongue takes to its whisking,
already the body warps thick with its muscle

as though I had paced this stage for a century, forging
the thighs, the thews, the vessel—but lovelessly,

lovelessly. I have no idea what variety of being
I may have been before, but it must have depended

on others too well, by which I mean, deeply.
Hot swallow of brine, must you further the thirst?

When I pince this tail, the century passes, I remember
the word for the curtains, *puce*.

2. AN AUTOCRACY ON THE LOUNGE

Because of: 1. this afternoon, this yellow smear of hours
(a) appearing like a yolk and (b) in bronzy autumn.

Because of: 2. the eggshell room, the chamber (a) in which
she lounges, (b) around the lounge, and (c) behind the picture window.

Because of: 3. the fragrant orange, which (a) a friend
has left her, (b) she peels, and (c) now peeled, approximates

perfection in her palm. It is for these she even bothers.
It is for these that she is royal.

Take the chintz alone.

How it folds: 1. around her,

and 2. as fields fold, its tendrils sprouting (a) a wealth
of green and greenish foliage, (b) a blue exuberance

of flowers, and (c) *in spirals,* she admires. She holds
1. a section (a) of orange, (b) among her quickening

fingers, and (c) against this fading light, then 2. her
eyes to (a) the fruit, translucent, then (b) the tender

seed within the glow. What voluminous and new
thought can hold her, seated, waiting to be borne?

She thinks: 1. *I am the seed, so nestled;* now 2. aloud,
in her domain, amending, "No. I am this *world.*"

3. THE QUEEN IN FIFTEEN COUPLETS

While the honeycomb alone becomes a feast,
One's best will number fourteen more in taste.

Be mindful; mind my honey do's and don'ts.
I have known ten dishes even honey taints.

Be shrewd; refuse the fruits of foreign lands.
Three figs I fed the king said PRODUIT DE FRANCE.

The margins of ermine may define
The limit of my robe, Love, but not my reign,

As the fruit which falls from heaven falls apart,
But an apricot of mine? Love, it never hurt.

The sixth opinion opened to dispute
Once, but shut posthaste. Kingdom Shut, my sovereign state!

As the leopard less its spots is still alive,
"I gave my all" implies "I have more to give."

On antelope: We pronounce one tame or wild
In accordance with the horn and not the hide.

Take sandalwood . . . please! I'll do without the grief.
Pedestrian scents convey, but not enough.

If clothing makes the queen, I am not myself undressed.
Pressed buttons on my organdy jubbah insist.

My tailor's fingers dripped in talent; e.g., they could stitch
A shantung parameter that would only stretch.

A waistcoat sewed the king could only shrink—
There are three French figs I'd also like to thank.

Four pounds of fish sublime now into thought—
The week in rainbow trout weighs twenty-eight.

Now summer vision ripens. Forecast: Deepest plum,
Producing chance of infinity in a little room

Streaked with Mexico, where every day, for lunch, I'd
Take swallowtail enthralled by vanilla orchid.

4. VERA ON ATMOSPHERE

Through the watery doorway. The membrane burst
which held the room at bay, and now this violet onslaught!
Impression first engulfs one turbulent as ocean, wine-
drunk wave-pursuant waves. —In a blinking, all the tropics'
harpsichord-crescendo prints upon the shore; it's love
in a rush of ruby-throated trumpets, shone to accompany
the pleasure of it spankingly. Assume a seat within
the rose of an open theater. That endless thunder flow's

your very fluxed induction, Peter, and you are   (*immersed*)
                  *   *   *

Take it in. As the purple vestibule became
ingestible by passing through, so the room

around becomes; the room a round becomes   (*immersed*)
Emit your little tongue. Take it in. Feel it

become you become it or want to. You cannot
comprehend unless you suffer to become   (*immersed*)
                  *   *   *

I have tried and failed. (She has misthought.) *Perhaps I miss the
principle or fail to embody it. . . .* —Now, disarmingly quiet on the
wide settee, its pigskin stained a true Aegean green, she contem-
plates a bronze—an Old World nudie, dust upon the wing. The
judgment? Otiose as a dose of posthumous opium. O, O, O—*my
room is overwrought! I am subject to excesses! I am a monumental
wince, an umpteenth sneeze preserved in Siena metal.* "Devise a
measure wise to follow," honks the philodendron, "and only the
passionate lunatic will transgress it." *Well, then, thank you. Adjust
my several senses. Pardon me, the very thought.* (She turns against the
hide, tomorrow: bombazine.) I am—as she is—wrought.
                  *   *   *

The doorway again, now solemn, gold, enters into the lobby

which leads to the room. Once it pounded upon you
with limitless force—once it threatened to kill!—but now

you withstand it valiant as statues stood under a dome,
still a marvelous dome. For beauty revisited, Stephanie,

is a mystery solved—yet still mysterious. Transcendingly
succumb. September dome-glow. Come where be   (*immersed*)

*   *   *

as a window illumes with an oomph seeping through

*   *   *

as a particle radiance seals from two; repeat, continue

*   *   *

Shades drawn down and drawn
closed the curtain.
What has one been doing? The lights

lay dampened down. Night's
smear on the forehead,
no more to be said. We have understood

and suffered in a room
which seemed often as not
an indelicate prison.

Where was beautiful
prison? No more to be done.
The glass knob turns

and now the door open.
Leave your last room.
Leave to find such a beautifuller one.

5. HER PALM, HER APOTHEOSIS
There—past the ghost of the carpet,
an inch from the tasseled fringe, an inch

from the froth of the wave
that plashed expressly

west of Asia; here—
in her isolate room,

in a permanent
pot of terra-cotta, its imperial fronds

outstretched, unfurled
in a fanning of afternoon sun, this is absolutely

the absolute palm. She sees
nothing else, no one else sees

the palm that she becomes, being
in a fanfare of vanishing, sun.

MAINTENANCE

How exhausting it is to be constructed
of a thousand parts—or is it several thousand?
Even the potato locked in the darkest
antechamber has a certain cunning, how it shoots its push
to the window's crack, how it sniffs about
for whatever, dirt. You know what I'm saying,
don't make me say it. It's too explaining.

Okay, make me. Make me that exhausted,
make me be conducted by the wind and back,
make me grease your several thousand parts,
say the antechamber is a part of something,
like a local chapter of an endless night. But I maintain:
even the potato togged in the sharpest
coat and hat, even the potato socked in the tender

you-know-what—what I am saying is,
in the antechamber, in the broad of day,
there are louver blinds behind the velour
hung down for the curtain, and it isn't right. It's too concealing.
I have always said: "Show freely to the world,
if not your worst"—and here I pause, enjoying nothing
half so much as a lesson broken, knowing

twice as many make do with less, and those with more
make too much noise, and it isn't working.
You have sent me pages of a close description
and it's very pretty, but it's too much noise,
and it isn't working. How exhausting it is
to be a doctor of a different kind, always
fixing false anatomy, an actor's doctor, always

singing. Now a bar or two from "Who's the Leech
and Who's the Patient?": (I can't remember.) Now
the famous chorus from *Days in Bed with Prayer & Fever:*

When I utter days, know knights will pass;
When I utter bed, know I never lie;
When I utter prayer, I'm a little believer—
And you know what I'm saying when I utter fever.

When I utter flew, I'm a Flexible Flyer;
When I utter web, I'm Compulsive Spider;
When I utter floated, make it nine to five—
And you know what's shaking when I utter wide.

—A dilapidation in the weaving room, call it cataplasia.
But I resume: "Show freely to the world,
if not your worst, yet some trait whereby. . . ."

Not a moment passes that I'm not aware of the degeneration.
The parts still fit together, true, but they are made
of breaking. What a glass of water on the nightstand
is your company. What a bedside manner, and you yourself
at least as sick as I ("the worst may be inferred").
On the open boat it was like lying down forever.
I had to close my eyes and open them again

to make sure I wasn't dreaming you. By the time the boat banked
in a nimbus of weeds,
I wasn't even breathing. Also, you were gone.
I see no way around this.
What I think we need—the sun at our backs like a drying agent,
our expensive tonics like a how-high moon.
What we think we need—it isn't ~~working~~ possible.

Two

SCARECROW IN MAGNOLIA

We raked until raking puffed our mitts with hot blisters.
Then we desisted. Wind de-raked our raking then,
spilled the tops of our piles, blew new-fallen bronzes

across brief spans of lawn. We worked like the damned:
I the Sisyphus of fall, you the Sisyphus of autumn.
Rakes dropped, we drifted through discarded wrappers

to a graveyard but yards from our unfinished raking, caught
neighbors peering down through parts in high curtains
to catch us there, looking. Oldest stone. Newest stone. Smallest.

One the size of a toaster read: *I bud on earth, to bloom
in heaven.* We drifted back then. With what leaves we could
muster we filled dungarees, a workshirt bequeathed

on a hook in the cellar. For the head: a plastic pumpkin.
And to keep this arrangement from the wind's
undoing, we cut utility twine in five measured lengths,

four for closing the cuffs, one to pass through the beltloops and bow.
We tangled these limbs in the limbs of magnolia.
The head balanced. Night fell. In the scant moonlight

and the light of seven streetlamps, the sealed magnolia buds
seemed a light silver, the peeling bark a lighter silver,
and the lesser branches brittle black. The figure shaking

in the limbs had shed its color, or it was also black.
The stuffed interior. The rumpled thing. The black flower
that we had meant to blossom was, blossoming.

ACCIDENTAL SPECIES

1.

Delivered here by hurricane, what path
a panic wind defined, abashing me wild
latitudes from what I would have been,
from bird beatified, bird fed; who am I now
who am, who in the violence of the storm
steered only in accordance—and was lost; who starts
disturbance in the flock; who is achingly
unreal, even to itself, and yet—who cannot help
but be gregarious; who twists a tense
black-banded neck, investigates faint song;

whose every contortion to avoid pain
makes more sophisticated pain; who asks
what is it now to hide what cannot help
but be divined; who has appeared now to itself
as a mechanism bound up to perform
certain functions, but not those of the clock,
which it had hoped to be, that it might
never notice how the spectacle revolves
around humiliation, a joke without
an audience; who was a plaything to the climate—

2.

I was a plaything to the climate, the breezes
lifted, swept me vast and plastic as they
wished, all eyes to my assignment from
the power in whose eyes all palaces, pyramids,
and the worms that build them are alike
contemptible; I was a humble ship set
hazarding from rock to rock, and on each
I struck a wreck, and all that changes you, confuses
parts for wholes, so that you become
the very swarm you would dismiss but can't

because it's you, united only by a drift,
a vagueness, an ability; knowing what I do
has to do with me, composes it, and by that
edict my paralysis decreased me to a mass
of tissues beating, void now flush now void;
I was, at last, an insect perched upon the wheel
of an immense machine imagining, able only
to envision its own inability, till inability itself
leapt through the silver gape of its laughter
and jagged back furious, with a persuasive aspect.

3.

The terror I had felt I would inspire.
Courted by the sweetest explanation, I gave in.
Design: The many wires of my throat.
They echo autonomically the piercing
gallimaufry of airborne undulations native
to this district. Not a trick, a function.
Accident: The longest chapter in the book.
"You've made an old mistake," said A, suspiring.
The agents lit the lamp. "Okay, I admit it.
But I only happened this way. I never—"

Design: The book is written. A means to say
"I never meant a thing," but in the fatal
drama of the gas explosion, the last three words
of A's last sentence remain—following
the author's unambiguous desire—forever
unspoken. Moreover, we'll never grasp
the wrench those hissing pipes were played with
or find the match behind that bloodshed.
Accident: I tripped. The rest was gravity.
Accident: Who, stumbling on a triumph, bellyaches?

4.

Acciaccatura: A grace note, that little
something extra. Literally, a pounding, a crushing.
Hear me mimic what I hear. However
strange the timbre, pitch or time of night.
—Love, in your presence, though it seems
essential to the gorgeous torture of my being,
I have never once felt. —I am by nature
made a mimicker, by miracle adept at taking in
and flinging back. —I have never felt once,
Love, that especially exquisite delight which

I have experienced in the presence of your image
when, ravished, my sextet has called it up
from the sensuous sea-chamber of my Mediterranean
heart with such magnetic music as would draw
the distant nightingale close: Love, so close
does it resemble that songbird's famous singing,
without, Love, the embarrassment of being.
Am I a criminal? Yes, of course. But only insofar.
It's cold tonight, cold and unyielding.
The forest's heart's a bitch. I mimic what I hear.

5.

What tedious auteur keeps changing
the scenery the minute it's established? What began
gaffed-up in the empyrean suddenly
zoomed down to gothic larchwood branches
and now dissolves to a cardboard city,
now closes in on one abandoned building's
lamp-lit window, now my winking eye.
Miss Singleton's *New Deportment Manual*
night after night proves indispensable, I cherish
our passages, they are not few, she says:

"Why not use appropriately varied tones of voice
so that each individual might best be able
to harvest the pleasure of your company?"
I do. Or I would. That is I will. I feel
relieved *and* anxious, as when discovering
the source of life's mysterious scratching
is a colony of ants beneath the wallpaper.
Miss Singleton, call a doctor. There is disease
about the mouth. It is ashamed of itself.
It makes noises that don't ever belong.

6.

If I only had a crutch I wouldn't wobble
half so much. What do you think you're up to?
Put it down. Put the phone down now.
Nights like this it suits me to wobble.
The water flows as in the homeland,
they can't get rid of it. A caller wants to know:
Is it still officially a murder if the dead
lived in a manner not found among those listed
in Dr. Singleton's *Complete Ways of Life*?
I cling polite by backyard bath, no stranger

to suspension on a low-slung branch, to blood
run burgundy, aflame. Persistent dread:
Dissimulation begets dissimulation.
Will we be the masters of the art, or its victim?
The African violet has passed away.
I am afraid I frightened it with my attention.
Or say the assailant is a mechanism
bound up to perform that particular function.
What then? A dozen sparrows thrash
one small delirium round the basin, blind to what I am.

The terror I inspired I am made to feel.

THREE PANELS DEPENDING ON THE HEART

1. KNOWN MINUTIAE

Because I could forever, my theatrical body
doubled over the bathtub estranged, a volcano;
might continue clenched in this arrangement

of numb white tile, white fixture, unfeelingly
learning, a bent apprentice to the pitch
of the wave of what mourning tows me along.

Because it is wrong, to know I should stop
but not stop, meaning: not push the urge
or act to conclusion, make good of my face and have faith

in her heaven. And because I am crude,
wanting anyone   you   to proctor this drama
however impure, I unlock the loud door.

I have known only minutes, known minutiae
of sorrow but not the sad hour, what such should amount to:
that crushed lids burnish a hazel eye green;

that the body, in shock, throws interior out
to consider itself in new aspects of grief
too sudden to count. I have failed part to part

with the heat of a novice. So father, be father.
Do difficult math in this doorway of air,
unhold to prepare me. Do not repeat how full is my

heart. Tell me   how   much must it part with.

2. WILLFUL TO SICKEN

Among mourners, she is stillest, a stone pillar
against the cruel fact of August, the slumped
animal heat of a summer worn out welcome,

out poppies, out purpose. In the window up front,
a saint floats solemnly, tongued by the flame
that will make him a martyr; nine cherubim poke

through the wreath of his smoke, at ease as he is
easeful at heart, burning. Whatever happens
happens, almost invariably. Even I know this.

And if I am meant, I am meant to keep calm, watch
everything unfold, cold as apostles—days,
nights, down in the shadows, devoted, fretless; an echo

banging on the eggshell vault—but why am I
almost always the opposite, swine from the bible
set loose and diabolical, a herd of my own?

I have felt what I feel form a swarm of contagion
reddening to pass through the pores of my face
and willful to sicken, to work itself into another—

I am not what I would be but know how I am,
willing her to pivot, to confront me
sloppy when taken to the trough of such leaf-green

grief that I can't resist. And when she turns
in the pew before mine, face pressed smooth
as the linen that proves her, I rise choked

through an incensed air, proud of my heart
because of what wrecked it, and prouder to infect
the one left living that would wreck it more.

3. THE TRUER

I will not give in. I will grow more strange.
I will wrap myself around your ghost till the ghost
itself wants letting go, till it shimmers free.

—And what an empty struggle. It'll only show
it wasn't you I held that way; there will be deceiving.
I've found my strengths since last we spoke,

and they're all tenacity; I've hitched to the house
as I would before, stood in the shade of your
stolid tree and wrapped myself around that, too.

I am not adapting. In a book of primates,
I'm the one macaque left clinging fast
as the others flee, all eyes and drastic

limbs and will, though the last acacia
falls to drought. When arboreal things
take leave of trees, or the ghosts of trees,

they slump in threnody. My hands are yours
that block it out, and we will never know it.
Though tussocked grasses bend and fade

in the risen wind, though the risen wind
rides its own solution. Though the planets fizzle,
I will not give in. Though deserts shudder,

supervene, I will grow more strange, and you will
watch that weathering. Crude in the heart
you once held delicate, creased in the face

you once turned from, frantic to practice
returning. Weakened, surely. But the stronger for it.
And the truer. You will not mistake me.

READING OF MEDIEVAL LIFE,
I WONDER WHO I AM

Every autumn, Walter, lord of the manor, ruddy
in his cups among the bundled stooks of wheat,
allowed himself the lustrous pleasure of allowing.
"Peter," he would start, nuzzling the russet
feathers on the head of his extraordinary hawk,
"I know you well. You are your master's, equally
cursed and blessed with the voluptuousness
of certain heaven-scented bog-flowers. Its extravagance,
if you will, is matched only by its generosity."
Peter twitched, remembering a swamp rat
confused in marshmallows. "Tomorrow, all the hungry
swine my serfs have dieted on air since March
will frisk about the turning labyrinth of oak
that is my private forest. They will feed there. I allow it."

Peter was at home, which was his master's arm;
Lord Walter left the field of wheat laid out
for ripening. By morning, word of Walter's
generosity had pierced the daub-and-wattle walls
of all the homes of all his serfs. These too
belonged to Walter, all homes did, and all the sleeping
serfs inside them, who were not their own—
although their drowsiness at waking was.
Through mist, the serfs conveyed the swine
to the lord's forest's border and released them there
to feed on fallen acorns; some ascended oaks
and shook nuts down into the chaos at the trunks.
Lord Walter would say, "They *clambered*."
He drank of his swine's music from a nearby parapet.

—I can't be Walter. I lack that confidence. I lack
that sense of intrinsic superiority, and I can't
imagine I would ever be at home with holding
claim to another person, much less several thousand.
I can't be Peter, complicit in all that, although

I would like being a bird, just not a raptor, except perhaps
an owl. I can't envision the serfs individually,
which is a real failure, one worsened by the fact that,
in this regard, they resemble oaks and swine,
gruesomely tusked in this era. I do see one acorn
in particular, panicked on its stem, and accordingly
I become it, shaken from my branch by a tremendous
hand and falling, never not falling—if the falling
stops, it will all be over. The swine will be upon me.

That evening, Walter, his custom since the death
of his beloved Constance, who died delivering
Christopher, the lord's first and only child, who died
in turn, it was said, of the selfsame grief
that overtook his father every twilight, rode
upon his sable horse to the cathedral, Peter on his arm.
There, against the gravity of vespers, Peter
quit his perching on the lord's leather glove
and flew in the cathedral, circling. The Adversary,
it was said, had claimed both wings, and they—
for the bird's sake—had to be removed, having
carried him higher than the elongated windows
which conveyed the eye to heaven and washed the cathedral's
limestone vaults and its innumerable pillars and

the outstretched wings of Peter in thrown moonlight.

MONASTIC

The ruined cathedral wept into my flesh
because I held nothing within me with warmth
enough to deflect it. I flattened a hand

against its relief to imagine the hand
that had carried it out—the cuff, the garment, the quick
scent of limestone struck into shape

and the whimper of cooling.
I carried myself with all I imagined
down to a lake, letting

are you   are you
loose over water, out in the air—
how incomprehensible

being has been to me
from the beginning—and back
to the rock, laying all of it

down—slant wood overhead
that would molder away,
the cowl, the calling, I can hear

the voice carried back to me,
lessoned, my own
blown voice, blowing   there   there.

PANSIES UNDER MONKSHOOD: A FOLLY

The sun broke: opportune. Opossum-stopped at twenty-two,
he cloistered shunt and jobless, kept to a kidney-
shaped plot of herbs, the medieval types (take rue),
a dense aroma-veil of beauties haloing the deadly.
The proximity of cure to curse, what blasphemy he knew
occurred in nature naturally (at once in scammony)
he honored; a clot of pansies under monkshood nodded
softly and obeisant, in pallor plotted, pallid.

God he gardened, darkly. Extraneous, neighbors stuck
an eyeball to a knothole wincingly and whispered
coarse outside his family fence. Whatever squeeze-faced critic
ridiculed, he heard—or overheard—or heard—
with tightening, what was said. He's catastrophic, look:
knot of inwardness and waste. A buttercup. A bird,
he feathered off from talk in tongue of other-mouth, dumbness
fledged into an art. See before him Francis.

See before him compost, a mound of it, the moist
rot monitored with heart. He makes a final tulip-hole
by hand, without a tool, and lays a bulb to rest.
(The cultivar: *Attila*.) A little blood, a little bone, a little
ritual accomplished heavingly and fast, the last
he'll know of company till March—maybe even April.
In the meantime: the basement. Dusty, misdefined.
Reading? He will read: left unoccupied, "the mind

rusheth into melancholy." Windowed, he will watch
an autumn's fancy branchwork, the crocus spitting gold-
dust stigma-tassel (saffron), but mourn the patch
of purple browning by the brick, the offal-air of mold
and loveless decomposing. Chiller nights approach;
blank acorns tap the minutes on a shake-shingled
roof with creepy repetition; the world he watered withered
into incremental desert, he drops: a rattled gourd,

an evacuated basket. Poor churl, he needs the solace
of a doll, a vacant entity to split his troubled
thinking with. Small wonder he should practice
acts of—what, exactly? A worsening, a cold;
a cold knocked back forever deeper into, he's
tilled himself an organ of perennial arcana, willed
root-veined rock from under underground.
He should finish applications, find a living friend,

not shear / *A decade before my first death I would lay me* / a shirt
of disconcerted madras taken from the mouth
of a cellar cedar closet—full spectrum, short
the violet / *askew on the bed of a dank room developing* / hues alive with
correspondence, he embryos a consort
concentrating deeply (as directed in his plinth-
thick copy of *A Pocket Book of Witchcraft*)
/ *headshots of those who would one day be wrung* / scissors held aloft

to catch the incandescence. For to fill it up:
the head's unstitched. For to eradicate the curse:
/ *null of quarrel and song, a whole roll of heavenly* / Rocky Mountain grape
starred "highly recommended." He considers,
but the range: elsewhere, noted. The buttercup?
Useless. Onward nonetheless. "Luck is got by cinnamon" but powders
though the cotton fragrantly and mocks him.
/ *shut favorite faces, dreamt photos to paste* / A singe of scheme

and mothballs. He wants the danger of November
night and blasted weather, its celestial, stark
/ *in the radiant album* / the grimoire flipped through: TRANCE, GLAMOUR.
Scotched. He backwards to the plot, the heretical book
/ *embossed with* THE GONE, *its* / rescue: an old grammar,
stammering, en plein air! Stood among the skeleton / *fluke*
pages turned to and bent over nights / stiffed in bone-
yard season, he / *creased* / "Puck, I'm here, in fern-wither, full moon,

in silent midnight, come—Your, believer." Silence, still.
/ *in a sea-toss and saturnine chanting* "alone, / He fingers lost delphinium,
thumbs the index down: WOODRUFF to WOOD SORREL,
WORMWOOD to WOUNDS. Back to WORMWOOD, his time
contends with him. / *alone,*" / The herb ends "small
bewitchments," soothes the bite of salamander, serpent. Some claim.
Burned by graves, raises "spirits who will speak. . . ."
Scotched. / *I abandoned myself on the false-bottom bark*

to belief I could grasp / Conjuring? A flashlight. He strips the brittle
leaves of artemisia off, a pinch of rue for mercy
should this business go awry, plucked laurel
for protection / *ways of grief by imagining* / in addition, "prophecy
through dreams." Watch: three o'clock. The double full
but only half, he circumspects a second: the granite's mossy
in the wall: a bounty, velveteen! He turns to MOSS
/ *all who would die dying well in advance* / good for "general-purpose

poppets," but for top results, you whet a "moon-washed knife"
and flense a "headstone's growth." Laid askew, awake
envisioning his visit / *each pang to the ventricles* / practicing a grief-
stricken look to throw the boozy gatesman, a classic
ending is contraptioned: "A pleasure sloop, a hidden reef,
and all of them at once." / *studied, withstood; each tragic*
scenario / The truth: blasphemous. / *pictured and stuck* / Anyway, the artifice
/ *in the propped-open book.* / comes easier: an uptown bus.

See before him Swan Point, the park of marble
monument and highbrow charnel. (His own are laid to rest
forever less exquisitely, capped with unremarkable
lawn-flush plaques.) He wheezes at the gate, walks past
without a word, but the pawns loom mossless—trouble

has been taken, meaning met again. A stiffening: exhaust.
Out of his pocket: an unknown key, an ambiguous token;

what weed

remainder's this? A quickening, a something

burning down to ash, for

"There is no happiness beyond an honest folly, for . . ."

—what, exactly? For he is eager for

THE DEAD:

BANGOR

It is true. Poor Aunt Midge, who: 1. refused to change
however times did; 2. spread (a) expansive memories
through Maine and (b) jarred orange marmalade on scones;
having lived: 3. equally for (a) pearls and (b) perms,
and 4. beside the phone, one longish life led out in Bangor,
one brain gone south like storm-watch bread,

has died. December twenty-four and "She is dead"
and we arrive. For nothing, it's decided, more will change,
not here, not up in rough and weatherbeaten Bangor,
where people keep alive: 1. tradition, and 2. memories,
surely as our aunt kept, up until the end, (a) her perm's
semiannual appointments and (b) a breadbox full of scones.

Here, best-loved recipes are not: 1. buried with the bones
of cooks, or 2. forgotten in their books. Here the dead
may die, but their good lives on, surely as Aunt Midge's (a) perms
still exist (in pictures) and (b) stranded pearls will change
hands every Christmas. We will: 1. swap, too, (a) memories
of our aunt—St. Anthony invoked—and (b) the Bangor

dirt; then 2. mark the passing of our hunger,
the little we admit, beneath a cairn of turkey bones.
By the fire, stoked, one may: 1. say (a) "Bereft of memories,
Midge was less than Midge, and worse than dead,"
so (b) "It's better this way"; or 2. cry, then 3. change
the course of time with (a) a vinyl treasury of perms

preserved in snapshots and (b) brandy. Both are worms
to robins wildered down in midmigration hunger.
That is what we are. We will: 1. have come so far, but 2. never change
by our design, for 3. find Bangor balm for all the bones
found "brittler each year" (a) up here, (b) in the dead
of winter, and (c) in semi-infinite supply, like memories,

etc. Will we become, as others say: 1. a flock of bloodshot enemies
embroiled over spoils, or 2. a tangling family of worms
that feeds (a) instinctively, (b) upon debris of their own dead,
and (c) till freed beyond the mouth-red boundary of hunger?
I do not know I am afraid. I pray Aunt Midge's bones
have bound us: 1. just as we are, and 2. from any change,

but when I pull the afghan up, I hear the chains
dismember, punctuate the dark; a whispering insists our enemies'
armadas are our own marred cells, our very bones
the bones of cinema, mechanically controlled. As cut worms
know, loss makes us us again, but in the image of a hunger
that we can't call back or contemplate or kill. We are that we are dead.

THE SPLEEN'S OWN MUSIC

1. PURGATORY CHASM

The earth has done this to itself. It heaved its rock
pectoral as an animal will, a brute mating. It must have
known that it would suffer endlessly thereafter

as the sea, reverberating, raised one steely claw, a second
and another: water's slow, erosive ritual.
That brand of love. The ghosts of razor grasses

watch from precipice and crevice, seething under
and above, swept hypnotized, as we are, by the shock
and aftershock of each anticipated wave. A minute.

A millennium. It's hazy, but we're here:
a study in repetition, breathing drowsy as the brume
we're watching struggle to disperse, particle

by particle, dulled by the hauled-out act, the redundant
sea and earth. Hapless would-be gas!
It's bound by laws of physics, laws of habit, laws

and love, love, love; the heat is overwhelming, but it isn't
our affair. We've traveled southwards
from the city, so ill at ease en route; you held

a radiant lemonade, and I the satisfactory radio
wired in my head: disjunctive music's drowning out.
Slaking still and still devout, we make a pair

in judgment, cast it everywhere but in; we both
approved of, once, the vista, but now it's harrowed out
the Sea Mist Inn, peopled the cliff with a pack

of naturalists. Wave on wave, this rite continues. Earth will not
recoil from sea, sea digs the deeper groove
we cut through others to inspect. A little closer.

Close. The rusted rail and sign suggest all
take precaution, be responsible. Shift in sediment
or squall can force the careless over easy—

and often does, we pray: the granting of the asked-for.
And look, I've grasped your hand. Spurred
by passion as before, I pull us near enough to drop

into the chasm, doubled over. An answer, an idea.
We want this want but turn, demure.
We are not alone. All the world is here.

2. NAUSEOUS HOUSE

The trains we will take will to take us down, to the sea
long sick with its suction of mollusk, its glares, its nausea

ours and no slip for returning, past spindled and torn.
A corn dog enters the mouth setting flares of nausea

off in the bellies that begged it, whiskey-and-soda
to slug them to sleep, then thirds, then affairs of nausea

wash from the day's damp bedding, or rather, pretend to:
strung out drying in vibrant air, there's our nausea

there, stained deep in the vaults of the convulsive, thumping.
As the boardwalks warp, the thoroughfares of nausea

rise underfoot, buckled with pumping, the lurch and stop
of our own Coney Island, where the cheers of nausea

egg us aboard, strapped in a whish of our own undoing.
We were suckled in distant parts, but peers in nausea

naturally converge, webbing each with each: freakshow
fetuses penned in jars, not knowing why (the seers of nausea

don't disclose) our world is rigged with too much charge,
splitting cantaloupe open, musking freight—in nightmares, Dame Nausea

carries me off to the Torture of Muscle, and I'm kinked awake. *But you
will never disgust me*—the stunned heart swears, and nausea

stoops to its quicker beating. Come follow me home, away
from what touches, threatens; let the snares that nausea

sets snap at our backs like the maws of spitzes lost to distemper.
I have founded a House, a room in arrears, where nausea

snakes from the pipes in a measure we can manage, sweet
in its way, a slow declining down the stairs of nausea

into the pit where the demons fiddle, but not for all ears—
such spinning, such music—of the nauseous spheres.

3. THROUGH A DARKNESS, AN INTELLIGENCE

On analysis, even roses aren't what you supposed.
Take a closer look, go deep enough to feel
that you're an aphid now, or smaller, a microscopic

version of yourself and delving in a velvet
den of quickened petals. That you were killed once
on some road trip you're at odds to recollect,

brilliantly ill-fated, numbered parts of you
removed, excuse me if I notice. You know that's what I do.
Also, there are more of us. A whole company

of spirits nests among this flustered damask
and delights here, accounting for that fragrance
one in ignorance ascribes to botany, a bland

and hasty explanation, but you see how it appeals
to Mrs. Osborne in her garden, who'd falter
if she knew the pleasure she derived from breathing

in her ruby floribunda's essence meant that,
for an instant, reddish beings had possessed her.
No matter that they're pleasant, brief

in overwhelming. Just leave her to her science,
what satisfaction it affords! You, however, asked me
why it seemed, just yesterday, a power

dragged you through a darkness, an intelligence
unbidden, surely not your own. You felt it
penetrate as thieves would sack a vaulted treasury

found long-since emptied out, cacophonous with spite, directing you
through frost and sudden blight and canker,
well beyond the lot of, for example, Mrs. Osborne,

who, as fate would have it, rose from breakfast at that time.
You approach me for an answer. I hand you
what you want. You have been given another life.

4. FOR A MISSING FACE

When to go would suffer me beyond myself, sloshed
in the stomach of an ill-upholstered coach

bound south, consumed, my will belittled
by the vast mechanic will of an engine lunging on,

the vent-shot air irrevocably soured
by surrounding mouths, spoil, my face mistaken

for a missing face, a general spasm down a darkened aisle;
when to stay would stifle as a vault of skin,

a masterstroke of disproportion in the woolens
worn, the vapors of a strange creation born

and breathed back in, as if to asphyxiate self
with self induced a more judicious choking;

when to choose would leave me *lost without*
or *lost within;* when the spleen's own

music rises, falls—I take to the air
as you took to the stair, my fled example;

when the walls streaked sallow
threaten to collapse, I will not give in.

See the one hand fixed to the gothic rail? See the other
hung, as though 'twere casual?

5. DARK NIGHT ON THE INSIDE OF A ROCK
Who misses the old days' stimuli, the nonstop
battery of matter, the beatings seen, unseen, the something

of an arm outstretched from Asia, the occasional
pinch of glass when he could walk but seven paces

to a new disaster's brewing, had been lying
on his side, digesting the disgusting, hadn't eaten

anything that wholesome for a week, and when he felt
the air grow heavier, then petrify, he welcomed it.

No way to cross the carpet to the light's too-distant
switch. No need to check the clock's diminishing alarm.

And when at last he woke, bound there in the dark
night on the inside of a rock, he counted himself fortunate.

Note: That much I remember. But the rest of the story
keeps falling away from me, almost like it wants to.

For example, how had he chosen that day in particular?
And when I try to imagine the look on his face, I hear

a jar of buttons cut from threadbare shirts. Buttercups
collect like cast-off thoughts about the border. I ask

for one last glass of lemonade, and I feel his boyhood hand
clutching a broken pencil, dissolving in salt water.

6. SELF EXHIBITED AS A WASTING PHOENIX

With each rebirth, a little more is lost. As pounds of feathers turn
to flame—then ash—an ounce, at least, is bound to blow off. Take
the breast. We trust it will appear less lushly plumed than myth
has led you to expect. Accept, please, apologies sung on our
tongueless bird's behalf. Do excuse as well: a slackened beak, two
dwindling wings, a blank expression. We've tried everything, with
no success. Worse, we understand the bird's interior faces identi-
cal risk. Medicine shows no effect. Transplant impossible, of
course. One cares to keep some distance between their person
and its cage. We find, this season, that our exhibit goes ablaze
increasingly, both in frequency *and* force. Sad creature of habit?
Emphatically, yes. For it's become quite clear that our poor,
wasting phoenix, of no more intelligence than the wood grouse or
pheasant, has yet to recognize the cause of its decay—although one
monocular theorist claims the opposite is true. To this hypothesis
our office has responded disapprovingly. Everyone's entitled, even
you, to speculate for oneself—that is the very privilege you pay
for—but our impartial charts insist that the bird's final flicker will
occur at noon, on or about the Thursday after next. A loss like
this will take some time to overcome—heartbreak and so forth.
Tickets available for those of interest.

7. EASE

Tomorrow I promise myself to be less contumacious
towards myself and not to thrash against the wheel

of my wishes that insistfully. The efforts of my flesh
to please my flesh will vanish as the rest of me

allows flesh what it will. Today a sudden shock
of grackles formed its mass upon the residue of what

was once my park. I hate that oily black; I hate
that plumage so bituminous that a match lit

under one wing should institute the next catastrophe.
But all I did was live. I listened to the body

bidding *live* and I indulged it. I know how to
keep myself on a bench. I know how to prune

in one fell pinch. I will be a flock of the feeding
flown. When one takes off, they all fly, done.

RELIEF IN GESTURES
ARTIFICIAL AND OBLIQUE

Risen again, insomniac, ungainly from a bed
of broadcloth helixed in a knot, and all the spinning
portions of my blood gone Hollywood with bile:

I know the blocking in and out, the hand held
stiffly boned, theatrical, inclined to shape some
portent in the bar of muscat light; I know what way

the head should droop, hypnotic as the pendulum
that took a mind to stop, and then another
to resume, the body subject to the dark, the shadow

phase of photosynthesis, when creeper climbs
the north of me, imperial and quick; when ivy claims
the south of me, riddling the brickwork, bringing

down the house. Nature is ridiculous. Once in a car-lot
switched with weed, I chased the partridges of Newark
and they ran as rodents run, roguishly mammalian,

headstrong not to fly. Sir Reason tolls, "You are mistaken."
The night is thick with folly, twists and false alarm.
It is my lot to be mistaken. Every ether's charm, I glow

aware of passing phantoms and aghast, a tendril tapping
at my pane with all the pomp of high occasion.
When convoluted in a slump, when shawled in big

exhaustion, when sleep should come instinctively
as flight will to a wing, I find myself in fits
of poorly rigged behavior, a little repertoire

I've scripted just to keep me, half-awake:
Now touch a match-tip to the wick. Now strut across
that glowy floor. Now play you are Vespasian,

staggering from emperor to god, upon your feet.
In an hour of affright, there will be those who'll pan
for comfort in a river of maneuver, who'll find

relief in gestures artificial and oblique.
I don't know how much I mean. There's a part of me
that thinks this need to lie is merely physical.

I lie now lying down, submissive to the vine,
allowing it to coil, wring and spirit off
with what weird molecule of life I may have

left in me. Nature favors ruin, and it will
leave me ruinous, the binding breaking up
the mortar of my cell and mortal home.

A doom runs through my family. *Now kiss goodnight*
as children kiss, mechanically, afraid.
The cloven votive falters; I know the close by heart.

(The cloven votive falters, spits and flickers out.)

Three

THE MONARCHY OF PAPIER-MÂCHÉ

The reign of the floor,
the necklace of lozenges
spindled and strung
on radiant wire, the scepter perfected:

no limit to what
he could make himself.
His orb the mantle
of a popped balloon.

A day and a half
devoted to the crown, its drying,
and the glitter's
appointment, the ceremony of making it

fit to the head
where the trumpets flourished,
where it all began
and kept beginning.

About his kingdom: There was no higher
site than being, seated there.
About his palace: There was no door, until the famous
tolling ripped one out.

THE DRIVER OF THE CAR IS UNCONSCIOUS

Driver, please. Let's slow things down. I can't endure
the speed you favor, here where the air's electric
hands keep charging everything, a blur of matter fogs the window
and my mind to rub it. Don't look now, but the vast
majority of chimpanzees on the road's soft shoulder can't
determine: Which fascinates more, the thing per se
or the decoration on its leaking package? How like us, they—

(The hand mistook me that arranged my being
bound here, buckled. I have been mistaken, ripped
from a wave of in-flight radio: wakened brutally
is brutally awakened, plucked from the grip of
"asleep on the slope of an open poppy." One has meant this
torture for another, clearly. Do we welt the same,
make similar whimper? Did he take my name? I'll take another.)

It is the decoration. By which I mean, we have a lot
between us. You're European, and I have been to Venice
where the waters pave and they can't play tennis.
Fair gondolier, it is my pleasure to confess: nor will you ever
catch me in athletic dress, hunched waiting at the net
for a ball knocked fast in my direction, hot with fervor
to knock it back to the opposing player. It just won't do.

Driver, please. I have shared with you. I have become
a person. That's supposed to make it hard to hurt me.
The future rises, bellows, wrinkles. I can't keep living
in a cramped sedan, I won't keep living in a cramped sedan—
though you hold the road, I'll give you that. There are
instances of smoke and mirror, instances of shouting fire.
Though you hold the road, I'll give you that, there are

instances of "sticking to it" that I can't admire, and ours
isn't an adhesion I ever expect to look back on
wistfully. But that's for time to decide, not me.

"Just around the corner, there's a rainbow in the sky."
—Haven't you ever just had to believe it? Look, if it's a cup of coffee
you're after, I bet there's someplace brilliant up ahead.
I bet there's someplace right around the bend. Ash in the eye

and the nose and the mouth, shit in the pants
and the mouth and the hand. Hound on the back
of the hand in the lap, slap on the face of the hound and the ass.
Ash in the eye and the nose and the mouth, mouth
on the nose on the face in the pants. Hound on the back
of the hand in the lap, shit on the face of the hound
in the ass. Ash in the eye and the nose and the mouth and

the mouth won't stop, it comforts itself, it comforts me.
Funny I keep on looking out the window, identifying
even as you do this. The orchids cry that yesterday were pollen
ground in the fuzz of dead-drunk bees. I will not submit
to being ferried that way. Driver, please. Where to now,
Tierra del Fuego? There is no travel but the travel that concludes
in shrieking with abandon, is there? —No. What you need

is to remember what it felt like beforehand, that emptiness.
Call up pictures, melodies, etc., but part of you will resist
that assistance, divide from it. Drag the edge of that memory—
yes, it's more like forgetting—across that divide, until
something like a rabbit-hole opens inside you. Vanish into the hole.
Vanish, it is your only opportunity. It will stun you
for another minute, but when the stunning passes, you will again

be nowhere, nothing, and even more at peace with it.

ANYTHING TO FILL IN THE LONG SILENCES

after Julião Sarmento: mixed media on canvas, 1998

1.

You have collapsed onto the table
I hold the table up. If I had a mouth
to speak it would be quieted (a felt gag).
An admired head of hair by now
it would be caught in the machinery.
Or any head at all there would be
hell to pay. Darling I have had
the most sumptuous idea it has
sustained me. A short fiction
I believe a myth I am not certain.
They have taken all my certainty.
Taken it and brought my Darling
to collapse. To have lived through such as that
has left one riddled in suspense.
That is to say, suspicion. Is it any wonder I refuse
to speak of Them more generously?
An August blue is a blue of assumption.

> *Together but distant,*
> *Together but distant;*
> *You're tied to the roof*
> *And I'm locked in the basement.*

Heave to! An architect is chosen
from a pool of architects. Do you remember
the feel of being chosen Darling?
With sleepless designs he excites a house
and the house is built, *tap-tap—*
miraculous! Do you remember the feel?
I am filling you in: my one true love.
The blueprints lie in a vault under lock
in time they will resurface. If the house
is simple it is also spacious I trust you follow?
The house is sturdy it will long endure.
This is the myth that has sustained me Darling.

A family is chosen from a pool of families.
The family lives in the house undisturbed.

> *Together but distant,*
> *Together but distant;*
> *You're tied to the roof . . .*

The house is the locus of no exception
no exceptional event. It assumes a history
of no "dark valleys" no "dizzying peaks."
The family is spared the hound of anxiety.
An astronomical blessing of course they
fail to acknowledge it. True it could—excuse me—
indeed it should be said that a streak
like this itself amounts—touché—to a blazing
exception. What I mean to say is nothing
such as that which happened to us here
could ever come to pass. No, not in this house
and not to this family. Fasten the cloud
for another century. *I took the fire for my mouth.*
They themselves must never imagine
so much as the ghost of the possibility.
I took the fire for my mouth, the blue-
tongued shudder as They slept, and it can't be given back.

2.
The architect is shot in the back of the head.
A precautionary measure the family
must never know. The builders too
a dozen identical shots to the head
each tragic but necessary. You are
familiar of course with that category Darling.
You have collapsed onto the table
I hold the table up. The myth continues
to sustain me. —And all the empty

lustrums flush so unapologetically, a single
wink of an enormous eye. You are
familiar of course with that organ Darling.
—And as the vault's locked door
springs suddenly open, the blueprints
spill to the cracked linoleum; and as cornets
strain from a hidden speaker, the divine
felucca cleaves the swell of a sun-flecked sea. . . .

—All melts under our feet, I know it does.
   Or else, the feeling that it does has cracked
Its ice-blue lily open, trumpet of innuendoes.
   I wonder what weird gardener would infect
The border's broadcast air with that aroma,
   It isn't—there, one hint of it out-dazzles the sweet-peas!
—Darling, I connect this to our drama.
   All right, I know. I make too much of chance, and always

Overdo my figments: I'm a reckless sleuth
   On a hopeless case, reading a strange flower
Marooned among the prose as some big clue to our mystery
   When there is no mystery, or when the truth
Behind it isn't an answer, or when the answer
   Itself cracks open, a shark-maw—but can it hurt to try?

3.

Heave to! Another identical house is built
but now in the evergreen thick of nowhere.
Note: Each of the builders of the second
—excuse me—I was about to insist
that each of the builders of the second descend
directly from the men shot dead
a century before, but I no longer feel the necessity!
How passionately I felt about that
detail a heartbeat ago how utterly

propelled by the beauty of it once.
You see that she is still capable of changing
anything to fill in the long silences.

Manitoba! Do you imagine it Darling
as I have always imagined it?   *Hush.*
"An untouched labyrinth of countless. . .
an expansive ice-lit theater of. . . ."   *Hush.*
The second of the houses belongs there
to be certain. I knew you would follow
my divine felucca. —A hundred years after
the first construction, an August blue,
the blue of assumption, and beneath it
the family's youngest, Tommy, hasn't "reported"
to the breakfast table. That isn't like him!
They call his name repeatedly over bowls
of breakfast flakes, or from the stairs' worn foot. . . .
A flash of panic fixing in a mother's eyes
is most arresting—*to repeat, to be certain*—
you have the next-longest résumé in panic Darling
I would be depriving you of everything
you have left if ever I failed to acknowledge that.

But who are those small—no, make that
Scarcely discernible—figures which float—
    Though I hesitate to say it—in elegant fashion,
Circling the lips of our brutal misfortune—
    Our circumstance, Darling, if that's what you call it?

In elegant fashion, with classical rhythm,
They ogle the aching we'd soothe but we can't,
    Circling the cracks of our drastic misfortune—
Our circumstance, right—in a dance formation,
    Flaunting their diadem, their cold ring of peeks.

73

Muttering faintly—I can't call it chanting—
They measure the aching but never reduce it—
   I don't think they can. They never attempt to,
But I think they might. You have collapsed onto the table
   I hold the table up. And in elegant fashion

those scarcely discernible figures keep dancing.
Heave to! We persist in doing what we do
and what have they to do with our drama?
They are not They. I would know it if they were.

4.
Meanwhile, Tommy will never answer.
He has been administered a smart narcotic
and taken away. He is just now waking
up in Manitoba in the house mistakable
in every detail for the sturdy home from which
he is now—and ever shall be—missing.
Imagine, Darling! Just like home, only
none of the people, every frantic look
out every window lost in an expansive
theater and drowned. We'll witness all
on camera, Darling. For I have always wanted
to watch someone else try desperately
to handle it. It might teach a person
about oneself and what it looked like happening.

> *How long I have longed*
> *To get that off my chest?*
> *How deep is the relief*
> *One gets from the voice?*

The battological moan of Canadian wind
cannot be stopped upon its lonesome
flight it can only alter as it hazards through

the various but limited configurations
of the aspen branches which the wind itself plays
a most remarkable role in determining.
The myth ends here. The remaining family
handles the loss until its edges smooth down
to the calm of a small commemorative stone.

5.
Tommy persists in Manitoba for as long
—excuse me—I was tempted to say
for as long as reasonable, but reason
has little if anything to do with it, we of all people!

What's that now? Yes it's violent,
radically in fact. I remember a power-
boat trip once, back in the misty
pong of my youth, high in a jostling
salt-spray boom, my throat relinquished
into the hands of an inward mariner—
or a skipper, Darling, if that's what you call it.
His anchor sank about a mile offshore
from a plum volcano the locals adore
from their shaken atoll an hour or four
from whatever the mainland happened to be.
Out on the ocean, there you can see
the violence embedded in the mere geography.
It works itself into the composition.
And I saw albatrosses glide about their business.

But whose are the hands—the arms, the thews—
    that lift the architect from that pool
in satisfaction of the myth's sad plan;
    whose execute him when his work is done,
whose hire the builders, hold the gun
    to their sunburned heads obediently

or with small compunction; whose discover
    the blueprints sprung from the vault
when a century's passed, whose build anew
    in cold Manitoba, pierce the needle
into the skin of the resigning child,
    whose carry it out, whose see things through?
—The impulse which activates must
not be reduced to a rational form!
That is, they are the hands that do.
They are less themselves in the act of doing
than in the fact of having done.

But why the passage of time?
The European starling, introduced
to the puzzle of North America
scarcely more than a century ago, now
ranks among the most abundant
of the birds of the continent, yes,
but a century is more than necessary, much,
to lift our architect from that pool
and execute him when his work is done,
to pierce the needle and all the rest.
Though female starlings favor mates
who sing most often and sing the longest songs,
a myth can happen in a thunderclap.
Of course I agree. But Darling you see,
that is my point exactly: why the passage of time?

—As happiness is measured out in freedom,
as freedom is expressed in terms of motion,
as motion is made manifest in time, yes—in time alone
will we, no—we will never be happy, unless—

FROM A FURTHER MEANING FADED

It will be shown that a departure demands that you exist
divided in two settings: (a) the one that it would break
your heart to move away from, (b) the other you have made—
in a vault of biochemical—arrangements to be visiting
in less than half an hour. And what a vivid, vivid day
you have dog-eared for your voyage! Notice how it rushes
up against the nervous thinness of your window, how the window
keeps its contract always to push it back, how colors
spindle off like promises misspoken on a platform of delirium.

It will be shown that your desire for an escort is the wish
to "negotiate" a path between the second and the first.
You cannot take yourself; I sympathize, I do. You cannot
talk yourself (not now) into another, into a final
desperate coffee when you really should be going, or is it possible
you can? The loveseat tries in dust to keep you
from your train, tragically repeating, "Stay, Christine!
You are not composed of steel. You are a crocus
so pristine that even valedictory hands discolor you with oils.

It will be shown that you deserve as many cups of coffee
as Bolivia can furnish." Rest among the lonesome
cushions for a minute, thinking, *This is where the real
meaning of Christine is always coming closer, almost into focus.
This is where the pleasure of it flowers if it ever.
This is where the threads of all the past of all the passing
merge about me in a poncho, a distant word for cape, possibly
descended from a further meaning faded.* All this time
you've been waiting in the station, and you only see it now.

It will be shown that you should see it. Shown that you should know.
Somebody somewhere monitors a doorway.
You have been expected. A seating awaits you, an opening
glaring as the serious ghost of an encyclopedia.
You belong there, gesturing, a corrector of flatware.

For when have you ever loved anything more
than to lay an item in the very place that it was meant for, really?
There's your romance. And today, Christine,
you are the very item. A scene awaits you. Will you accept it?

It should be spit-shone, swellegant. For what a summer afternoon,
"the most beautiful words in the English language."
That's a quote of a quote of a quote, Christine.
Can you trace it back to the original mouth? To the mouth before that?
(Mournfully the weather turns rather violent.)
It is the mouth you walk through, tooth-pulled, fucked.
This isn't the stop that you meant to stop at.
(Mournfully the weather has turned rather, hasn't it?)
Somebody somewhere gives up altogether,

and your heart pitter-pats, your machine skips a beat.
Show me you know what I mean when I say
that throwing your body to the sidewalk doesn't make the doorstep
come any quicker. I know from Broadway.
And the half an hour that it always takes
to drag it back up is a dreadfully long thirty minutes, hear me?
The way we suffer, there's just no music in it.
Not anymore. Though I wish things had ended
differently between us; between you especially.

Presto! I don't have to show you anything else.
Let a stranger do it. Let him whittle you down to a shadow in a park.
Let his music exhaust your stinky little orchestra.
For what does it mean, to be "meant for," really?
I was meant for production, but I lost myself on the Hudson River.
I am speaking now from that selfsame river.
Let him carry you down. It's like that dream
where you're stood in the rushes, christening the flotsam.
The flotsam's life is all departure.

I am speaking now on behalf of the flotsam.
And this is where the pleasure of it flowers, Christine.
There's a touch of oil on every hand.
But what does it mean, that the stranger says he's pure Bolivian?
He speaks like a sparrow hawk, dichromatically.
He says if you wouldn't mind a travel south.
And if you wouldn't mind swallowing a measure of ocean.
And of course you wouldn't. And of course you will.
Rest perfected, in a meant interior Christine, dissolving.

DELPHINIUM

We didn't mean what we had said, yet very happily
that much was understood, so far as we could see, beneath
the canopy we stood beneath both after and before

the formal ceremony, where, wanting something new to say,
we said how beautiful the flowers were, although
there were no flowers there, only memories of flowers

flaunting blue remembered beauty, which, being disembodied,
wanted something like a sentence to secure it.
So much was understood, we really didn't need to say

anything but wanted to and did. Moreover, all that beauty,
disembodied as it was, wanted something to secure it,
so far as we could see, beneath the canopy we stood beneath

together half an hour, between the food and music.
Later, in the evening, both surrounded by those flowers
and unwilling to admit it, we wanted something new or

something newer, a form of filling in a crust, we said
how beautiful the canopy beneath which we had stood was,
knowing, as we did, eleven ways in which it wasn't.

—But when the rain began to fall too heavily upon us,
when the rain became too heavy for us ever to withstand,
we found ourselves, again, reflecting there beneath it,

the canopy beneath which we had understood before,
understanding, as we did, beneath the shelter of that canvas—
where the memories of flowers and their flaunted

beauty haunted us, admit it—that it moved us, brought us back
beneath a happiness, that place where we could call
something beautiful and not mean and, moreover, mean it.

KNEELING MAN WITH CANE ON CONSTRUCTION

*After Bill Traylor: poster paint and
pencil on cardboard, 1940–42*

Tonight's full moon's a circle pressed mechanically.
It speaks to the cardboard's first purpose, a mystery.

Or, supposing the drawer didn't *draw upon* but *drew,*
the moon's the tracing of a coin, or whatever round you

imagine. Encompassing all possibilities is impossible.
Always another surprises, as once a shock of purple

knocked all of Alabama to its knees, and then it
vanished. A top-hatted man's a girl in a bonnet

whose good dog's pizzle drizzled its deliberate
puzzle in the earth, with dignity, as Jesus did, albeit

with His finger. Those occasions where you listen
so religiously you end up wondering if the lesson

isn't all the noises made, but all the ones left out,
are not, I repeat, your fault. Nothing is ever anyone's fault,

for the word implies that fissure put between
the one and every other, which is to say everyone

must be responsible, has to balance like the kneeling
state and stay that way, always knowing *wrong*

isn't the word for the unbent positions, rather, *poor* is.
The man whose mouth's a rupture in the purse

through which the money spills is just beginning, poor thing.
He considers beauty in the way a dog does cooking:

around the clock, but not as action—as an object only.
Leave him time to even. In the evening, purses empty

out as all things empty out, heaved back into the water
that feeds the moon in flower. Never hurt anyone, ever.

AN ACTING APPENDIX

The Haunted Wood may be rendered successfully by a minor company. However, should time, purse, or the actors' tempera-ment not allow for the performance of the drama cap-a-pie, which is to say, *as written,* then the story of the love of Steve and Fanny, or of Buck's carousals with the river phantoms, will, we believe, make for a diverting—albeit brief—night of entertainment. The point, of course, is never to exceed your resources. The former "playlet" is made up of Act I Sc. ii, Act II Sc. iii, and Act III Sc. ii, up to and including "This shouldn't hurt," and may or may not conclude with the masque that crowns Act IV. The latter is made up of Act II Sc. iii., Act III Sc. iv, and Act IV Sc. ii, from *Enter phantoms, dizzy* to the end of the scene, omitting the sacrifice or substituting stalks of foxglove for the moon-lit blades. The masque itself makes a charming distraction, especially in cities where "traditional dancing" is still appreciated. (Rest assured: There is an audience for almost all productions, even the most rudimentary.) Let Mr. Bishop, Dick and Candace call up the masquers, as in the uncut play, and let Steve and Fanny witness it. Begin with a passage from Mr. Bishop's speech: "Is it me, or is something arbitrary?" Continue to the end. After Steve has answered, let Mr. Bishop say, "No, not that. Something bigger. *Much* bigger." Devise a dance for Candace. Let her dismiss the masquers with slow, mysterious, and persistent movements. Cut from "I don't get it anymore" to "Will we never be satisfied?" Continue to the end. Cut Mr. Bishop's words about persistence, concluding with "I am tired of pretending."

Note: The number of phantoms should not overwhelm the stage. The desire to include the entire company should be resisted, or what is meant to be beau-tiful becomes confusion.

HIS LONG IMPRISON'D THOUGHT

1. IT IS NOT THE MAN WHO HAS TOO LITTLE, BUT THE MAN WHO CRAVES MORE, THAT IS POOR (SENECA)

Maidenhair borders the upward trail,
trims the margin braided green
and lives here—thrives—in the dark
beneath these arches, in this

chancellery of pine. The mulch
of shaken leaf and needle showers down,
is dampened black by runoff:
the debris that feeds the fern.

I hazard up the path
and pick a wayward frond.
No life should be so simple.
Fern sucks upon its nutritive

and never wants for more, flaunts its weave
of leisure. I cannot call it good—
although infusions ease catarrh,
and thrown on glowing coals

it imparts an aura of protection.
I smear the sample in my hands,
pray the stain will satisfy. I said I'd make it up
the mountain, but I can't believe

that I (apart from any humming).

2. COLD TRIBUTARY

All day long, the cold tributary whirs: black water
through bracken, through pine. I have pitched
camp aside. Riverbed rocks and the firs dropped in

make the creek make a background or more remote
hiss. It knows nothing but furthering on.
I have come to consider this. Sun overtakes

far lavender peaks, embosses the campsite
in larkspur and rose. It dismisses the racket the water
releases; I recall little when, I thank goodness.

Nature has its place here. Roadside weed
flowers elsewhere as flowers picked for tisane.
This is how well I can be. Hale high noon,

I climbed the blue ridge and descended
the same, kept turning the rack
till I chose the right pin, the proper memento.

More like me than myself. I am making good
use of my time. When night pounds down
this immaculate campground, I buckle in quiet

as everyone must: no rustle or squeak from
my little lean-to. I have washed myself off
thinking, *Only the creek here is meant to continue.*

3. MAN IS A REASONING ANIMAL (SENECA)

The crow cries because hunger is no
lovesome way to feel, today or any other.
I correspond with her. I am panoplied
in feather. In the distance, orchards grow

decreasingly as pickers basket apples.
They polish some for market, press
the wormholed into cider. I cannot look with ease
into the face of strangers eating

or in any way at home—at peace—
with satisfaction. Countless feet before me
pounded every trail flat. The gratified
go speechless; I don't know what I have.

Well below the weedy precipice, over
the edge of the present mountain,
the stasis of a pond encourages blank algae.
I comprehend miasma. I read once

of another. They fished her body
from a river bent in prayer. Pond growth
shrouded her remains anonymous,
a farmhand had to break her to fit

into her modest, designated coffin.
I figured out the squirrel's fury
only yesterday. After all the nuts
are gathered and the nest is built, what then?

O crow cry. More nuts. A new nest.

4. SWAMPLIFE (HAWTHORNE)
"A freshwater brooklet flows towards the sea.
Where it leaves the land, it is quite
a rippling little current; but, in flowing across

the sand, it grows shallower and more shallow,
and at last is quite lost, and dies
in the effort to carry its little tribute to the main."

—I battened me down to weedless a shallow, to pure
field of widening pool. The salty pull of
ocean pushed, and I stalled myself—on purpose.

I wanted no dilution, no brackish suck
to sea. And the waves have failed to touch me since,
and an age of waves has failed me. Death

is distant, welcome wash. It is not my term for this
daze of sludge and swamplife, the turgid
mass of peepers I have become a home to, am.

Moons in mist, I dream of the terrible rhythm.

5. IT IS A ROUGH ROAD THAT LEADS
TO THE HEIGHTS OF GREATNESS (SENECA)

The switchback stairway
makes the walk up easy, but
I am breathless nonetheless.

Worn faint in my habit, I pause
in shabby light, on a birch stump
mossed for no (seeable) purpose

only minutes from the rocky top.
I witness the woods as they hide the face
piecemeal, spattering footprints

in cone, stick and needle. Come occasional sun.
I am frozen how I am—thinking of a time.
A cloaked man held me, an obedient bundle

of five years, wieldy, over a guardrail printed in car-crash.
It fenced the length of a bridge with persistence.
Below me, the frantic water rose swollen and cold

with late-winter snowmelt and maybe I asked for this.
His arms dystrophic, I shook in a peacoat I meant to
keep still. Otherwise I would. What little I remember.

I looked indirectly but never away from the swallowing
river, to remember, I feel the cold gray of concrete,
of jarred animal brains as they give under scalpel.

6. DREAM
The stream turns out to be sourceless so the search
for its origin ends among pinecones. Here one continues
to decompose, here another, another, and there:

a fresh one falls, a fresh pinecone falls soundlessly, lost
in the ceaseless push of black water. Most loss is expected.
As this is a forest, so this is a forest of loss and of losses,

four shoes now sink in damp numberless losses, needles
and leaves that decay and decay. Preferring a blur, I swallow
my glasses. A greyhound arrives with a fiddle, singing:

> *Our eyes adjust, in April, to filigrees*
> *Of budding maple, to daffodils aburst*
> *In soft through obstreperous yellows.*
> *We forget ourselves.*

> *But by August, if not sooner,*
> *All our sweetness is exhausted,*
> *And we crave the snows which suffocate*
> *The business in the meadows.*

                —Suddenly December.
Snow has fallen and continues to fall. The crickets
have long since been silenced. I watch as my vision

becomes an environment: the branches bare, damp air
hung still. This is my season. Here is my element.
The greyhound again, now producing a monocle:

"Do we appreciate the bleak—or bleaker—atmospheres
because they speak (a) to us directly, like mind
to mind, as in telepathy, or (b) in tongues that tickle us?

Do we sing (a) the most pertinent, heartfelt hymns, or
(b) ridiculous requiems which merely turn our thoughts . . . ?"
Turning from the water means turning from the dog

stood in the dead-angled stalks of bankside yarrow
to be done with it. Out of my pocket, another pop quiz:
"Months ago, about a mile downstream, four hands

picked two heaps of flaxweed and yarrow and shaped
with ambition twin poultices to expel a shared pain.
Answer: Whose hands? What ambition? Why pain?"

7. IT IS BETTER, OF COURSE, TO KNOW USELESS THINGS THAN TO KNOW NOTHING (SENECA)

My foot dashes on the next to last
rock but no angels, no crows rush
to bear me up cowering. Complete
with score for trumpets? It is not written.

Winged creatures have no charge
over my physical body wounded
or body free of pain. I cannot imagine
how "succor" must feel, how a toe

can flare so astoundingly hurtful—
from the fat knuckle downward
to torn ragged nail—and keep on
hurting. Better not to have read

how good God had it than know how
but not have it too. Otherwise I

89

tend in my way—by which I mean after
a fashion—to be faithful. Blood

drizzles earth from the insole
of sandal, but I will move upward
as though unhurt. *Rudbeckia hirta*
straggle nearby; a lost half dozen

resist the seed and season, direct
black eyes to a sun of indifference
however it nurtures. Daisy know
nothing else. I find this variety coarse

dumb yellow. The sun of course
lacks all opinion. Standing nearer to it now
than ever before, I will breathe
the air thin of its dizzying vista,

the earth stretched out before me—
touched fiery, complaisant green
for the most part. I think less of oxygen here.
Let mountain be inverse of gorge

or abyss, offer me all that below.
There is no enough, and I want
what is not. Which way should I walk
now I know how I never will be?

8. FALL IN SUMAC (CAMPION)

The broken bones are one thing. Physical fractures.
Mendable when held immobile, healed when given time.
But this is altogether different. I snap a branch

from a drift of staghorn sumac shrub in passing, work
of scattered human hands. *The tender graft is easely broke.*
And how I bear it like a wand: a solid tuft of reddish

berry tips the bobbing end. I knew an urge once,
acted on it. My summer nature overcame me. A spell
of bliss upon the porch, below catalpa, in a heat.

O never to be moved. I splayed as earth and August
pinned me. Some would not be fixed. I am superior
to plants; I am a king in this capacity. Berry clusters rise

to pay me homage, rust to ruby. On occasion, rose.
I gesture to them, there. It is a pleasure to be
noticed. *It shall suffice me here to sit.* Darker now, I know

this isn't my domain, not mine alone, this printed
old embankment. Thistle sunset. Spurge and vetch around
my ankles. Tethered sloop in far-off harbor rocking

as the sea rocks. *So cleares my long imprison'd thought.*
Wrest off as many branches, butcher as I will,
another flush of leaves will come and cover up.

Yet stubs doe live, when flowers doe die. Soon I will forget you.
The broken branch will be replaced and fruit.
The sun will spin the wheel. *Know buds are soonest*

nipt with frost. The sun will spin it round again.

BIRDSONG FROM INSIDE THE EGG

As meteors pierce the sky's tin vault,
so molecules sail through the many

pores of my own enclosure, what trash what
treasure, piss and brilliance, a fleet of

snippets shed from the vast exterior's
chaos haystack, flop and fodder, there

is no NO, not here, not yet. I have been
forever, I am not yet born. Into the one

tremendous whistling laze of this, my
pulsed amalgam, I admit the all, a just lie

back and snap! arrangement, confetti
hoof and concertina, what blind mouth's

breath what pleasant nesting. I am
a composition, the one life's work I have

been forever, the loom and the wool and the mat
for dreaming. The song that's tensed

in past as happened "just like that" is
too much once, and lying back to bask in basking's

tongues of flash, I can't believe it.
One's quarantine's a peace pinched-in

with heavenly visits. A heavenly visit
has no close. Take the most exquisite

moment in the gallop, where all four
hooves now tread the air, and stretch it

taut indefinitely, shot through as it is
with hops and dung and does and loves,

and you have an inkling. An inkling sparks
half the congregation when you rub it right,

half the congregation when you rub it wrong.
I am song forever. I will not have sung.

NOTES

The epigraph is taken from Wittgenstein's *Culture and Value* (Peter Finch's translation).

"Twenty-seven Props for a Production of *Eine Lebenszeit*": "*Eine Lebenszeit*" is German for "a lifetime." The poem adapts a line from Edna St. Vincent Millay's "Recuerdo" and another from Alfred Jarry's *Caesar Antichrist* (Antony Melville's translation). This poem is for Richard Howard.

"An Inflorescence" borrows two lines from "Eileen Aroon" by Gerald Griffin.

"Sonata ex Machina": A few passages in the poem have been adapted from Thomas Hardy's *Jude the Obscure*. The poem also owes a debt to John Singer Sargent, who titled one of his paintings *Carnation, lily, lily, rose*.

"Der Nachtschwärmer": The title is German for "The Night-reveler."

"Marblehead" is named after Marblehead, Massachusetts, the "birthplace of the American navy." Some phrases in the poem are adapted from the Marblehead Chamber of Commerce web site. Others are taken verbatim from Aeschylus's *Prometheus Bound* (Herbert Weir Smith's translation), G. E. Lessing's *Laocoön: An Essay on the Limits of Painting and Poetry* (E. A. McCormick's translation), and T. S. Eliot's *Four Quartets*.

"Fanny Fowler's Poetry and Dioramas Workshop": The epigraph is taken from "Bella Donna" by Stevie Nicks. The poem borrows from Henry Wadsworth Longfellow's *Evangeline*, and the indented stanzas owe their form to John Keats's "Ode to a Nightingale."

"Maintenance" adapts a sentence from Samuel Butler's *Erewhon* and quotes another (in pieces) from Nathaniel Hawthorne's *The Scarlet Letter*. The poem also owes a debt to Alfred Tennyson's "The Lady of Shalott" and to William Wyler's film adaptation of *Wuthering Heights*.

"Accidental Species": A few passages have been adapted from Herman Melville's *Moby-Dick* and Charles Maturin's *Melmoth the Wanderer*.

"Nauseous House": The author wishes to acknowledge that he has deliberately smudged his ghazal.

"Dark Night on the Inside of a Rock" takes its title from a line in Henri Michaux's *Tent Posts* (Lynn Hoggard's translation).

"Ease" is for Mónica de la Torre.

"The Driver of the Car Is Unconscious" takes its title from a lesson in *German for Beginners* by Charles Duff and Paul Stamford.

"Anything to Fill In the Long Silences" adapts a line from Georges Bataille's *Evil and Literature* (Alastair Hamilton's translation). This poem is for Lynn Melnick.

"An Acting Appendix" owes its title and much of its form to a guide to performing low-budget productions of *The Tempest*. The brief how-to, written by Evelyn Smith, appears in Richard Wilson's 1923 edition of the play.

"His Long Imprison'd Thought": The lines by Lucius Annaeus Seneca come from his *Epistles* (Richard M. Gummere's translation), and the Hawthorne passage is from his *American Notebooks*. The lines by Thomas Campion are excerpted from the lyrics beginning "Though you are yoong and I am olde," "O never to be moved," "Loe, when backe mine eyes," and "Sleepe, angry beauty, sleep, and feare not me."

"Birdsong from Inside the Egg" take its title from a poem by Rumi.

ACKNOWLEDGMENTS

Unlimited gratitude and love to Lynn Melnick. A heartfelt mountain of thanks to Mary Jo Bang and Richard Howard, the shepherdess and shepherd of this book, and also to my teachers, especially Peter Sacks, Elizabeth Spires, and most especially Lucie Brock-Broido. The number of family, friends, and colleagues who offered their support and advice throughout the writing of this book is too great for me to thank them individually here, but my gratitude to each is no less profound for their being (my fortune) so bountiful.